COYOTE BLUES

Free Verse
and Prose Poems

JOHN
GARDINER

5/23/13

For my dear friend,
Yvonne —
Best Always,
John Gardiner

WindFlower Press
A Boutique Publisher
Orange County, California

Coyote Blues
Free Verse and Prose Poems

Published in the United States of America
by Windflower Press, Orange County, CA
Box 7089, Laguna Niguel, CA 92607

Previous publication information about some of the poetry contained within this work can be found in the end pages under Acknowledgments.

Books in Print.

ISBN: 978-0-9889709-0-8

Printed in the United States of America on acid-free paper.

First Edition

Cover and book design: Jann Harmon
Jann Harmon Design 949-291-3977
Author photograph: Pamela Fish
Editorial/publishing assistance: MaryAnn Easley 949-285-3831

Coyote Blues: Free Verse and Prose poems; walkabouts; other sentient beings; heart, soul, spirit; mixed bag; poetry about travel, environment, nature, love, loss, life, death, connections, animals, human frailty, aloneness, spirituality, solitude, earth, universe.

Contents

III Heart/Soul/Spirit

IV Mixed Bag

I Walkabouts

The Cats of Leningrad
for Anna Akhmatova

January 27, 1944

Pyotr Markov had survived on a few grams of bread, more sawdust
than flour. He made soup from rotting mutton, joiner's glue,
leather belts, and calf skin, the stench of which he never forgot.
He put pine twigs in hot water and called it tea. He chewed on
raw soil near Badayevsky, where fires after German bombings
had melted sugar from beet crops into the earth. He pushed aside
bobbing heads floating in the Neva River when he went for
water. He read Pushkin's poems to the children to distract them
from hunger, and the theatres remained open even as his world
seemed ending.

May 9, 2006

Walking with thousands of Russians through St. Petersburg (no
longer Leningrad), in commemoration of Victory Day and the
end of the 900 day siege and over a million lives lost, I watch
Markov quietly celebrating in his tattered war uniform, drinking
vodka, eating brown bread and pickles, face weary and peaceful,
wrinkles dug like trenches across his forehead. I ask my friend,
Olga, about all the statues of cats tucked away throughout the
city, and she tells me: *It is our way of honoring them, thanking them
for their sacrifice; they were the last of the food before we had to eat
our own dead. Troy fell. Rome fell. Leningrad did not fall.*

Enniskillen

As I take my seat at the William Blake Pub
in Enniskillen, drab working class town
not far from Belfast, home of my Irish roots,
the first thing I notice is Samuel Beckett
staring at me from a framed poster
announcing his centenary celebration.
A man next to me is carefully re-rolling a cigarette
into three, one for each pint of Guinness
he explains, and he asks me what I'm doing in town,
where I'm from, and I'm watching his smoke
curl around the stern visage of Beckett,
hanging on his thick eyebrows,
and I answer him,
"why, I'm waiting for Godot."
He says, "he don't come to this place,
he probably goes to the Catholic pub
across the way."

Californian

At mother's funeral, a first cousin said to me,
"We're the older generation now, the story tellers,"
and I thought of my travels with mother
up and down the coast from Eureka to San Diego,
camping in lower Death Valley or high in the Minarets,
the boring grind up the 5, childhood dreams
in Grass Valley, Nevada City, passing Shasta,
strange mountain of cults and deities,
our stops at Conway Summit, highest point on 395
between Canada and Mexico.

Sometimes we'd sing to while the time
and she'd tell me which tribes lived where,
the history of mining, stories of the Cornishmen,
and all the names of trees and flowers.
When her father rode his horse across the state,
he hardly saw his feet for two full days,
so thick and tall were wildflowers.
He never got the pollen off his boots and pants,
or so the story goes.

Driving south, headed for the great basin of L.A.,
thinking of five generations of Californians
I carry in my blood, stunned by the endless
proliferation of cars, panoply of metallic colors
brighter than the sun, my old slow truck
plodding like a plow-horse,
nothing but autos where the wildflowers were,
none of their names worth knowing.

Rio

From the fourteenth floor of *Hoteis Othon*,
the white-gold sandy beach
is a quarter moon freed from sequestering skies,
nestling now on the starboard side of Brazil
where rhythmic waves and their humming sounds
curl from jungles on her northern tip
to Ipanema's drum-beat in the south,
the shore break so evenly drawn
on Copacabana's coast
it's as if I'm in a ship, high in a cat-bird's seat
headed out to sea, to south Atlantic mysteries,
half-necklace shoreline fading behind me
waiting patiently for her other half
to clasp,
and all the diamonds in the sand to shine.

Kano to Cairo

The Sahara desert rises from below
like Dante's vision of inferno, and the plane
shakes like an elevator with a faulty shaft.
Prayer beads rattle, the engine coughs,
and out of nowhere, staring up in horror,
nomadic specters from the pock-marked sand
struggle with sacks of colored glass.
Are they a Berber tribe with Goulamine beads,
this far east of Morocco?

I can see the whites of their date-colored eyes.
They are a ghost battalion made of roots and scrub.
They are too close.

United Arab Airlines, Flight 107, is going down.
I will die in a dune—my bones will blow away,
scraps of calcium for hungry mice.
The Muslims are whispering to Allah
and juggling beads as if they were white-hot.
We're going to crash, and it's my fault.
They stare at me—the hideous, hairy hippie
from the West, day-glo dashiki, purple pantaloons,
green slippers with toes curling up like mutant weeds.
I look like one of Ali Baba's thieves.

When we finally land, they impound my passport,
seal me off in a small room and stare—
not in fear or anger—they just want to know
why I was in Ouagadougou and Bobo Dioulasso,
Mopti, Mali, of all places,
and what I'm doing in Cairo
with a weather-beaten, expired ticket to Frankfurt
and five dollars to my name.

Togo, West Africa

Thunder clouds rumble over the rainforest,
dark bombers loaded full,
lightning tears through sky,
heaven opens its spigots
and bends back the jungle,
sculpts pock marks on the old mosque—
waves scale palm trees
taking fronds and coconuts back to the sea.
I drink malted ale, dance with African friends,
daybreak opens like a cave—
we pound on drums, trying to keep time
to the bass notes of the rain.

Los Trancones

On the coast of Los Trancones,
Mexico's garden needs so little care
it's as if the vibrancy of salt air's
enough. Succulents and perennials just grow.

Yuccas, agaves, and century plants
stand like elephants,
roots thick as trunks,
white tepals flapping like flags on green tops.

When days are sweltering,
iguanas soak up sun on flat stones,
ancient symbols of verdure,
prehistoric dreamers from maternal swamps.

Just like Rwanda

Some countries have death and mourning,
and not much more, apparitions in the cobwebs,
hunger encroaching like desert sand
spiraling through the jungles,
eating everything that's green.
Channels of death are choked with children
caught in riptides of useless birth.

All the mad tyrants spin deadly dreams,
weaving thread from flesh
and stacking bloody coins.
It is so obscene and yet runs free.
Death ambles with ease, sucking fresh blood
with armies of mosquitoes in tow.

In the land of Timbuktu,
the throats of youngsters are callus dry,
and Sahara heat sears through scalps
like light through glass.
The tiny ones die of thirst, rot in the streets,
there aren't enough flies to go around,
just another story in *The Times*.

These people die better than anyone, they're the best.
They cash out like casino chips,
and compassion's credit has run dry.
We're dealing with familiar bones and early graves,
not spiced lives loaded with luck.
Death sops up waterways
and makes deserts of us all.

Pockets of Tangier

Just off the boat and wading through Tangier,
shoulders down, arms crossed like a fullback's
on fourth and one, passport and money
tied across my chest like a bandolier,
I lash out at the hands all over me
with my elbows and knees, and still they rip
at my pockets, scratching for loose change
even as I try to beat them back.

The stout, red-faced German in front of me,
screaming in his native tongue,
casually kicked a small boy smack in the face
with his heavy boot, and the boy,
blood streaming, was right back
undeterred,
seeking anything in the pockets
from the West.

Ramadan

In the medina of Marrakech,
a man sells hash cookies
to dreamers.

I sit on a prayer blanket
stoned out of my gourd
and bow to Mecca,
downcast eyes
redder than Holy-War blood.

My ministrations are insincere.
I think of girls
and islands,

searing image
of a gorgeous lass,
dress caught by the wind,
flown upward like a kite
before she could recover.

Her legs have followed me
all over the world
through thirty countries plus.

That sly wind,
those long legs,
meditation on prayer mat
long forgotten.

L.A. Night

Night falls on *La Ciudad de Los Angeles*—
planes descend on tartan tracks
skid of brakes, hiss of smoke
smell of rubber musk,
rush of cars from valleys and hills.

Night stretches her arms
and balances the stars—
the big city pulls them to her chin
like a shuddering child
with a warm quilt.

Angels settle in, vagabonds write songs,
stars shine from sidewalks of fame.
The ground below L.A.
continues to move
and the planets spin away.

Macaws of Laguna Canyon

Free from the grasp of clumsy masters
and rushing through the gilded gates of cages,
out the windows they fly, joining scores
of emancipated parrots, massive beaks
cracking carob shells and squawking in unison.

Nature's inexhaustible, and rainforests will return.
Sycamore, oak and eucalyptus will branch out
and make room, as originals usually do.
Green wings are floating through the canyon
with Amazonian memories
and South American songs.
Soon, the river will return,
and chapped hills will swell
with strange plants, broad leaves,
jungle flowers.

San Francisco's pulling us north
with her slave moon and willing tides,
and everything south
is following.

Reno, Late December

Indian summer day, silver-blue and warm,
1999 rushing in between storms,
lenticular clouds over Tahoe's snowy range—
one has a triangular rainbow
like a prism.

Katharine says, "It's an ice cloud
evaporating in this glorious sun,"
and I think if glaciers melt
on a day like this,
I will stand in my backyard
embracing tidal waves with a smile—
go ahead, let the clouds vanish
and the waters rise.

Walking the Marin Rim with an Old Friend
for Bob Currier

Up a steep slope, down a deep gorge,
we walk the grades and valleys
from San Raphael to Fairfax,
green grass and oak trees, sycamore,
tufts of thistles purple as a King's robes,
redwoods up above—
volcanic strata, igneous rock, streaks of diorite,
dolomite facades formed from a thousand quakes,
thousands more to come.

We trudge along spouting Shakespeare
to Druid faces in the rocks,
quiet soothsayers measuring history
in ravines, rings of trees,
layers of sediment.

Here we are, four decades of friendship
singing in our footsteps,
each of us an aging Sisyphus
pushing stones of time.

Gold Country

Chopping up scrap cedar and slow burning prune
for the wood stove, I watch finches and juncos
eating catkins from the birch,
and I think of my ancestors
who watched blue jays and hawks
in a forest knoll near Lowell Hill
close to the Immigrant Trail.

They saw wagon wheels hanging from tree limbs
like ornaments, twenty feet off the ground
after Spring melt. Now, except for logging roads,
nothing else is there—
just high wind
and deep roots.

Summit Lake
July 20, 1969

Up here at Summit Lake,
10,000 feet high,
the moon shines
like a butter lamp.
Up there in the black,
men walk for the first time;
I stoke embers for more heat,
small fire cracks a twig,
thin gray column of smoke,
green tea steeps.
I read Suzuki by red coals
and stare at the cold stars.

Lightning on the Mountain

Walking switchback trails to Tuolumne
under fast-gathering clouds,
lightning fells a pine just up ahead,
loud crack and a shiver before splitting
like a boiled shell—
I heard my dog howling
as he raced down Camiaca Peak,
fur buzzing like a nest of electric bees,
lightning bolts crashing after him
hot sparks nipping at his paws.

The World Below

Down from mountain's top
to the crushed rocks beneath
where boulders die,
rucksack balanced, boots sinking
in scree, leather scratched
by scrabbles of shale,
the sun's a climbing eagle
and I'm under its spell
gazing at *topo* maps for a trail—
makes no difference
which one I take,
they all lead to the world below.

First Growth

Leaving base camp at eight
after coffee and trout,
walking switchbacks through saxifrage
lupine and sage,
we head for the ridge where dwarf pines
cling, weathered trunks
sunk in volcanic ash.

All this green life
came from fiery gas—
explosions in space
generate flowers.

Mystic Arts Bookstore

Mr. Police Chief and fellow cops:

Where were you

really

when the bookstore burned down,
when Mystic Arts
died like a Viking?
Did you get
Timothy Leary
for good

or

were you hiding
in the smoke,
thick
    as thieves
burning rubber
up the coast?

From the Haight
San Francisco, '66

Headed for a concert at the Avalon on Sutter and Van Ness—
Airplane, Grateful Dead and Quicksilver, patchouli and pot,
thick freezing fog, brain cells stretching like cotton,
hit of blue dot shifting gears as I float along sidewalk,
taste of baking powder, colors mixing like a broth,
better get a grip on the saddle.

People pass by disguised in flesh, mouths gape and flash,
mutants and cave dwellers! My thoughts careen
like squadrons from lost imagination, low and off course,
stringing clouds together like bouquets, trying to grow wings
over the wind and glide home free as a paper plane,
and beautiful girl stops, smiles, hugs and kisses me,
gives me flowers, tells me she loves me, moves on.

And everything is changed! Sun comes out bright and clean,
fresh as after rain, and she turns around at end of block,
smiles, as I did back, and I went on to hear music
dreaming of love, thinking of her, tripping into the gloaming,
wishing I could have said something.

Subway Sting

On the IRT late at night, three young kids
maybe 16, scheme how to mug me,
one shows a gun; somehow,
I have the upper hand, I'm feeling malarial,
shivering, dripping sweat, eyes blood red,
mosquitoes once again in my veins,
and I unwittingly defuse their plans
like a munitions man guessing which wires
to snip on a bomb—my delirium's confusing,
they stare meekly at their feet,
predator pretense slinking away,
rattling out window cracks into tunnel rock
and screeching rails; they exit quickly at 96th St.,
people pause before entering my car,
give me furtive looks, think better of it
get on the next one.
I shake away lonely as a leper, no one gets near;
my tokens spread virus, my eyes carry fever.

Window

Outside my barred window on the edge of Spanish Harlem, my street level studio hole, dimly blinking like a holding cell, the whole world happens: Sal's Pizza, Chinese laundry, Greek Deli, Latvian tailors, Salvation Army, Baltic glass repair, Swedish Triple X, Thai food, flea market, Irish bar. The homeboys on my block sell skag and speed, and the worst weed in the world. They're in a Puerto Rican gang called "The Sandmen"—they got chains and tattoos and attitudes, they got leather and scars and rap sheets, and they roam their turf wearing steel-toed jackboots—and one night gunshots rattled my window frame, heavy heels thudded away, and there was a "Sandman" right outside my window with a purple mask where his eyes used to be, framed by the shadowy bars, his face and head blown apart, but I couldn't turn away—bits of brain and skull bone were scattered like white rice in pools of blood, blood everywhere, spread over heaped trash bags and garbage cans where he lay sprawled; and he was shivering, in the throes of contortion, and for a second under the moonlight, a river of blood seemed to wrap around him like a cloak, changing his clocks and closing up shop in the sudden factory of death, and I watched him mutate under the lunar sky. I saw his soul row away, pulling through the river of blood with stolen oars, like a mutinous sailor—I saw it rise over Harlem like a guiding star. I watched the blood coagulate and cling to the empty husk, the dead shell. Garbage men didn't touch the bags or cans for weeks, not until a mountain of trash covered the spot, a sort of second burial. I told the police I saw nothing, heard nothing, no one had, and they didn't press me, they knew another body would hug an enemy stoop in a few days a few blocks away, and it did, on Amsterdam at 106th, it was so predictable. That was the language of the smoking throat, where bullets talked in tongues. A few years later, I moved down Broadway to mid-town, where dreams were broken quickly, people walked like speeding cars, no one stopped to pick you up, no one gave an inch, and no one told the time.

Back to the Sea

In late August, we hike to a shady bank
on the south fork of the Yuba
and attend to our task,
releasing the remains of father
and brother into the water,
James Francis and James Robbins,
ash and carbon rippling on the surface,
souls drifting free—

a marvelous liquid cloud, white as bone
slowly stretches out,
green phosphorescence shining through
lit by algae from the creek bed—
minnows, dragonflies, and a garter snake
bear witness, we share a peach
and drop the pit into the stream,
seed into seed
father and brother winding together
down Sierra tributaries
slowly to the sea.

II Other Sentient Beings

Coyote Blues

Man keeps a razor at his cheek, scissors to his scalp
hangman's tie around his throat,
runs on two legs plus four wheels, eats meat he hasn't cooked
and doesn't need, his belly's more than full.

I pulled over in the canyon, traffic speeding by,
got out of my truck, hauled a dead coyote
off the road, people honked and screamed,
"Get out of the way!" Did they think I took its life?
I hope so—at least that would explain their hate.
"You can't do that." "Development might stop." "We can't care."
"It's just a mangy scavenger." When I tried to get back on the road
no one yielded, so I got out again and lay down next to coyote.
I played dead while autos whistled by, no one stopped.

I asked coyote who would hear his cries in the night and he said,
"Only the blazing moon."
I pledged my love to him and to the animal world.
I dreamt coyote dreams, slipped into his skin, brother of wolf,
cousin of dog.

I have run with them on four legs in a wilderness of dreams
eaten what I needed, thinned out the mice, worshipped the moon
howled with the goddess of open space and water holes
sniffed the ground and searched for my old friends, the Indians.
I wonder where they went—
                         they must have been hit by cars.
I am coyote, four-legger, straw-colored fur, survivor
        so far.

Best Friends

In early morning,
I lean from a sink
to touch wet noses
with my own,
and dogs lick water
from my dripping face
as if I were a cousin
with food to share.
I stare into pools
of dog eyes,
sleek coated canines
filled with patient trust.

I wear enzyme
of dog's tongue
on my skin
and never wipe it off.
It is magical,
the stuff of ancient times,
drawings on cave walls.

It is the stuff
of resplendent dreams
in my animal mind.

Shadows of Themselves

After killing all the animals
& developing all the open space,
they tried to flush out
God,
who had taken the form
of a field mouse
in a tiny thatch of old scrub.

They used shotguns with chemical scatter,
thinking it good sport,
& were certain they had Him,
but God escaped.

He slipped the noose
& staggered away to His own
scorched earth nightmares,
overwhelmed by toxins & depression,
stunned by the unrelenting
greed & violence
of these weak creatures
whose own shadows
were too frightened to follow them.

For a Raccoon

Beautiful raccoon
dead by side of road
so peaceful looking, softly asleep
on your journey.
I say the Diamond Sutra for you
Buddhist prayers
Indian chants
Christian hymn.
I write
some thoughts, a poem
for you
to mark your passing.

God be with you and your family
and thank you so much
for marking my heart.

Dogs Know

Dogs know that if answers aren't simple,
questions have no worth.
One dog, ancestry unknown,
rescued from death row at the eleventh hour,
had been a vagrant in the alleys of L.A.
living on pavement scraps.

Now in luxury's lap, spoiled as a Sultan,
he takes nothing for granted, circling like a clock
from twelve to twelve at every meal,
pacing as a man in a cell would, counting steps,
dropping bits of kibbles at various stations of time,
two o'clock, 4, 7, 9, and 10.

Dog is clockwork efficient when it comes to food—
even after eight years, he fears abandonment.
Later, returning to his bowl, he's delighted to find
supplemental food stashed for emergencies.
Man didn't touch it, never has—
he shares food with dog, but asks for none.

Dog feels lucky—there will be flowers in the Spring,
bumblebees to chase, scent of raccoon,
treats in his bowl—loving hands to lick.

Backyard Jungles

When darkness locks like a holding cell
and jail bars writhe like snakes,
when breath is short and humans don't understand—
visit backyard jungles,
lie down with dogs and dig for seeds of memory,
dream of elephants who pass the bones of elders
from trunk to trunk and sadly reminisce.
Study love with canines.

When lonely as a mourning dove that's lost its mate,
never to mate again,
gone to a grave of enduring drought,
turn again to dogs,
umbilical links to instinct, scruff-haired angels
at your feet; always turn to dogs
because wolf and coyote won't come near,
and the moon's a lonely beacon
with no ships left to steer.

Coyote Talk

In canyons where metal shadows roar through, coyote's imperial corridors are waning. Doctor of Wilderness, please find a remedy. If anyone has an elixir to slow the beast of progress, bring it forth. We're losing spirit guides—coyotes are lying on roadsides like shining premonitions of a black future. Coyote pups strain to learn the conversation of pavement, sniffing and reading the history of the world and wondering why so much is covered. Coyote says we must cook with dirt if that's the only way we can respect it, taste the un-skinned meat of death mixed with the salt of bones. He says that everything is shrinking—terriers were timber wolves once upon a time. Doctor of Wilderness, please kiss the snouts of dogs. Their ancestors approached our fires thousands of years ago and patiently waited for scraps after helping us hunt. Free the pangs in coyote's mind, release the banished tribe of wolf. Let the world know there are more living organisms in a handful of topsoil than there are human beings. Savor desert winds, bay at waxing moons. Please do these things because coyote asked for you—he said there are no poisons worth making, no animals worth hating, no trails if we continue to cover them, only what's left in our mutilated wake.

Dove Hunt

At 14, hunting with father
for the first time,
20-15 vision compared to a hawk's,
excited and nervous, ready to aim
the 20 gauge—

suddenly, doves!
Shotgun up and sighted
easy shot
         missed—

impossible!

And yet I hit
my heart
with unseen pellets

and knew
as sure as shotgun shells
that killing
was for someone else.

Migration

On the west coast, nasturtiums and bougainvillea
are sprayed by gray whales
breaching close to shore
and singing of Alaska from their corridors
of salt. I climb aboard with barnacled palms,
slide down slowly, grip their slippery flukes,
and skim the lunar sea.

We spout and plummet together, trading forms—
we become the source of all things
in our iodine mind:
red tides, subterranean swells, spawning songs,
millions of silent years in these waves.

Pelicans

High wind and tumbling rain, pod of orcas off Laguna coast,
quick walk with the dogs between storms,
damp winds rising to the clouds, waves of pelicans
drift south following the Pleistocene shore,
the ivory necklace of foam curling like a map of the world
when seen from above,
and they're drifting directly overhead,
and when I look skyward, it's as if they're floating
down a river in a long skiff,
supremely motionless, flash pictures in an updraft,
and I'm gazing up from the bottom
like a wide-eyed fish anchored in mud,
another drowning man
searching for elysian wings.

Swimming to Catalina

With yellow dock lines
tangled in his antlers
like a crown of thorns,
the young mule deer
swam to Catalina
dazed and wounded,
surrounded by jet skis
and harbor boats with horns,
all well meaning
but a ghastly scene
to watch...

If the white tailed buck
hadn't died
from open cuts
and certain trauma,
I suppose
they'd have released him
on the golf course,
where the last
wilderness
used to be.

Coyotes Cry When Great Spirits Pass
for Dr. Wilderness

They had never been seen at the lake before—there was not
enough ground cover, and humans made unnatural paths for
metallic machines that smoked and rattled, choking life from
flowers and shrubs on either side, motors that seemed to cut an
ever widening swath, carburetors with oily dreams of flattened
mountains and tire tracks under every sign of the moon. There
were stories told by coyote elders of humans who could read
the wind when it whispered through pine boughs, who knew
that the sound of rivers had changed with each slight thaw of
snow pack, who accepted coyote howls as spoken verse. There
was one such man known to coyotes as "King" because he ran
on their grounds and spoke with them even when they could
not be seen. He had howled when his mate was terribly ill,
and coyotes said his echoes circled the stars and changed the
plane of evening light. When his mate passed, coyotes said they
watched her leave in a beam of moonlight, with three stars and
a purple meteor slowly leading her. Her smile had freed a canyon
overgrown with brush, and a dormant stream returned that had
been dry for a thousand years. Several coyotes could not contain
their excitement, and they ran to the lake, a forbidden place, to
tell the King the great news of his mate's miraculous smile and
wondrous trip through ether and cloud. They had never paid
tribute like this before, and when six coyotes sing to a two-legger,
their song remains his forever and will reverberate when he most
needs to hear it. They cried in unison before running from the
King's cabin because coyotes always cry when great spirits pass.

III Heart/Soul/Spirit

Rewinding Time

I surfaced from the dark tunnels of a western swell
and crashed on a third reef break.
I live in a house of termites
that shakes when the big sets roll in,
and I pay my dues in salt and rust.

All my life I've dreamed of tidal waves
when grandmother ocean will muster her molecules
and obliterate shorelines.
I have no fear, it is a cleansing of sorts—
wood structures will quake on their foundations,
steel bolts will fly away like birds,
and whale bones will rise from the desert floor
to welcome the water back in.

When the surging swell arrives, foam saddle on its back,
hollow sound of wave-wall thundering like a stampede,
insects will dig down to dry shelter
and humans will float on emotional seas
circling like the globe itself,
wrapped in kelp, feeding on plankton,
wide fish eyes staring in wonder
at the backward moving sky.

Defilers

(Headline: Toll-road agency itching to build on burned land)
"With rare gnatcatchers dead and their habitat in ashes, there's
no reason to delay San Joaquin Hills toll-road construction
through charred canyons, county toll agency officials argued
Wednesday."
—*newspaper story, 11/93, one week after an arsonist destroyed
Laguna Canyon.*

I tell you, man, you defilers of land, canyon fillers, despisers
of green shrub and oak, despoilers of old growth, you asphalt
worshipping, less than senseless things with concrete feet
and gloss-black shoes tied with the guts of cats, you sellers
of fast roads and fast gods, you with hearts of cash; I tell you
that outside your closed-door, high security locked gates and
chemically treated shining rugs, there are magic plants and
trees, wild weeds that teach coyote verse and habits of the deer.
You don't understand what you are paving: leaves and flowers
to combat virus, herbs to cure depression, potions and elixirs,
roots chewed by primordial tribes. I tell you, man, your belief
is a sham, your progress a lie; your friends are craven, your god
is a coin, your books are blank—you are one-eyed jacks with
shadows for skin, oil in your veins, and a slimy deck of cards
from which you shuffle. You do not recognize the church of
earth, the great spirit, open land, peyote gods of astral travel. You
believe in endless breath for a million generations just like you.
I tell you, man, you're in coffins already, pink-stucco-repetition-
townhouse-living coffins, locked in a carapace like a sow bug,
but the worms will find you, your accomplishments will melt,
and you will be a long slow dinner for the maggots of eternity, so
please, please soften your real estate eyes and examine your legacy
of shame. Otherwise, your sad, sterile children will dig up your
bones and scatter them for the crows.

The Apple People

He ran across the pastures under a waning moon,
freaked out on LSD or STP—he wasn't sure.
His head was out of fuel, he had no reserves
to cope, and when he lacerated his ankle on barbed wire,
he came to a bloody halt in our front yard.

The apple people were behind him, he screamed,
bobbing on stick bodies, oozing worms and black decay.
My mother came out, agitated and blinking
from deep sleep, sized the situation,
lay down next to him on the grass, held him gently,
sang nursery rhymes—and we talked him down
all night, slowly placing the apple people
back in the orchards from which they came,
reuniting them with young pippins
or whatever else it took.

In the morning, he roused himself and shook
like a wet bear, peeled off the layers
from his chemical night,
and sailed the surface of a new day,
ready to paint fresh colors
on blank canvas skies.

Loneliness

Loneliness
is much colder
than winter's bloated coat
of ice
hanging on the stable door
in the far corner
of the old pasture
where no one goes
any more.

First Born

There are brilliant memories we can't decipher,
wind in the jungle, cave fires, whispering rain,
forgotten sounds, metaphors lost in our breath,
and whether we let go on our own
believing we're gone forever,
or continue the teeming cycle of birth and death
makes no difference.
Directions are useless, language conjured.
We haven't even figured if the stars just glow,
or beckon.

Misperception is everywhere.
I am here, you are not, until another time
when we'll cling like spores
to reproduce,
yet honey bees were fathering flowers
millions of years before we came,
and perhaps they speak to us in the same way
that angels do.

Nature urges, blows us to and fro.
No matter where our spirits decide to shine,
paradox has always been the first born child.

Both Barrels

Love for any time at all is worth the price you pay to fall.
- Fred Neil

When there is neither rhyme nor reason
for midnight incantations,
and your sloshing words crest and die
like melting cubes of ice, you remember a time
when the sea shone like quartzite
in a small boy's eyes.

Words are broken shells
that can't be repaired,
you live by yourself for years
because you've run out of havens
to search for or believe in—
sometimes you call friends at the witching hour
and read poems till the birds sing,
and sometimes love hurts so much
you consider eating glass
when the bottle runs dry.

When love and money disappear for years
and time stretches
like a strangle cord,
you want to banish whoever said
good health is the most important thing;
when you have neither love nor money
good health sits on your shoulder
like a mocking bird chirping near a sewage drain.

Sometimes you remember the color blue
has many subtle shades you never gave it credit for
and pain is not only relative,
it's a first cousin.

She's gone—
you peck at a keyboard as if letters
become seeds, and you must grow something
in a blank expanse of alkaline sand.

Sometimes words get stuck in your throat
and you don't know whether to reach in
with one hand and remove them
or use the other hand
to choke them out.

Sometimes, even death doesn't seem enough.
Release was never guaranteed and failure never leaves.
Love is double barreled, but one shot's all it takes—
love can dig a graveyard, take you by the hand
and lead you to an open pit.

Iridescence

Sometimes, sighing and groaning,
gazing at the waxing moon,
iridescence swallows us whole.
It must have us both, but the light holds you
closer than a microscope.
It bathes you, molds you with kinetic fingers,
wears you like an aura,
and when you emerge, like an oracle
come to life, spread like a treasure map
of cheekbones and hip curves,
everything is revealed.

Sometimes I feel closer
to secrets of space and time
than any pilot
shuttling through the sky.

Love Exits Stage Left

The sea is bleeding in our eyes, waves are backed up for miles,
corrosion lines our cheeks, our sockets are tide pools,
the sand around our mouths is like a beard.
Dogs lick our faces with rough tongues
digging for salt, enough to season meals.
Look closely at our faces, you can swim here.
We're confessing—love is gone again—
words change, but patterns never do.
It's night time, it's lonely.

Our angels and lovers were cut off at the pass,
and now they're around us, pitiful souls from purgatory.
Their screams are silent, but we can feel their breath.
We can't carry this weight—you flip it easily in your fingers
like a baton. We bear it strapped upon our backs like humps.
Look at our shoulders, they're caving in,
they're moving into our chests like squatters.
The bones in our arms are dueling with our hearts,
balance is losing ground—we must become amphibious
and swim away from our heads. Please drop a baited hook
and lead us to a stream—apologize to Love,
she hasn't returned our calls; leave our eyes
next to the door on a plate, I know that bothers you,
they never close, they're watching for our next move.

Black Swan

If Love comes pulsing like a south swell
in rain pelted jungles of my heart,
palm fronds slick as enamel
blood hot as fire,

I will take off my clothing
and bathe in moonlight like a child
awkward and stunned—
layers of loneliness will vanish,
gauze will clear from my eyes
like clouds releasing the sun.

Love has nothing to do with feelings,
it's tangible as a coming storm;
there's one road we're born for
all we need is a footpath—
if I can walk with you,
the ground will be there
even when the road is lost.

Drowning

I'm writing away from you,
and this is a death sentence.
These words are row boats, the race is on.
I must pull the horizon close
with phantom oars, drown memories
many fathoms down, forget squandered love
listing on the shore.

Appeals are useless,
tears disappear like old friends.
Perhaps I'll see you again,
perhaps the sea will speak.
All bets are taken,
winners get paid off in salt.

Single Heart

Loneliness is so quick and devious,
she breaks bones where no bones
should have been, her surgery's exquisite,
no splinters, no anesthesia
numbness settles perfectly, by the numbers;
no heel-prints on the heart or massive loss
of blood.

It's her development that hurts
year after year
as she outgrows the clothes
you've dressed her in,
demands food from the cupboards,
drives friends away
and lifts your sheets for the winter wind.

You live with her under one roof
separate as snowflakes,
measure her in rings
like the stump of an old tree—
if you don't give her fresh bones
to gnaw on,
she will suck out all your marrow
without breaking skin.

Act III

When he finished his part in the play,
hanging at the end of a rope,
there was no curtain call
or *denouement*,
only a desire to leave the stage,
discard his costume,
& transform—

Freedom was in a noose,
music of the spheres
in the sudden cranium of the circling sky;
he was like a caterpillar
so eager for his wings
that he jumped from the green branch
still wearing his cocoon.

Psychoactive Connections
for Jerry Garcia

A thousand assumptions are made about me
as soon as I drive by—
long gray pony tail, Dead stickers,
Nature Conservancy, Save the Canyon,
coyotes, wolves, bears and Buddhism,
a veritable book of information
stuck to my old truck, too much to take in
unless you're stuck behind me in traffic
and have the time to absorb what drives me on.
The teenager who I'd picked up hitchhiking on PCH,
just like me 30 years ago, long dark hair, tie dye,
eager for the next corner turn and what it might bring,
says to me in dead earnestness,
"I really miss Jerry, man. I was gonna see 'em at Tahoe.
Hey, did you see 'em on the grass last year
in Santa Cruz? Wow, outrageous, totally."

I told him in dead earnestness that I hadn't seen Jerry
since 1966 at the Avalon or Fillmore, with Quicksilver
and the Airplane, which were the bands I'd gone to see,
the Dead holding much less appeal.
His eyes narrowed and he looked at me
as if I were a narc, and suddenly I became his Dad
in the cab of my truck, cooler because of my hair
but just as distant, probably ready to pontificate
about what I did when I was his age, and the distance grew
and my coolness shrank; in fact, at least 30 years
vanished instantly in my rear view
like highway markers
announcing all the turnoffs
I no longer took.

El Niño

Strange light, as if the sea, lit by blue gels
were a stage floor—
storm enters from the south, hurricanes
cue the ninth month, mammoth waves
on Brooks Street,
eight-footers from trough to crest—
surfers ride the crease from third reef breaks
parallel to shore,
two blocks from where they paddled out.

I pick at words
like a man scraping barnacles
from the hull of a ship,
stare at a blank page, dumb as fog,
and listen to the constant sea,
marveling at her choice of sounds.

Waves of Sound

As I take in the sound of waves
night after night
on shores of my dreams,
close enough to the sea
to wake with salted lips,
as if I'd been caressed by fish
or felt the kelp from a lapping tide
dragging its evening tail,

I feel the breath of stars
from empyrean spheres of fire,
and for a moment
I'm between the blue tides
of everything
like a wandering dreamer
beached alone in space.

All We've Forgotten

In the black witching hour,
    I don my sorcerer's cap
and all colors, even those unknown
    seem feasible.
This is the hour when *Peace*
& Love glide across gemstone seas
silent as glass figurines.

This is the hour I send prayers
        in a fleet of paper ships,

sails flapping like Tibetan flags
skimming over secrets in the deep,
    mysteries leased to all of us

where everything is possible,
      yet rarely understood
if ever found.

Everything Under the Sun

Cracking open a piece of shale
from the flats of Utah, I find
a perfect fossil of a trilobite,
first invertebrate form of marine life,
no larger than a dime and long extinct,
an arthropod that dominated
the seas 540 million years ago,
moving across the sandy bottoms
in search of food.

Now it has worked its way
into the 21st Century,
and like everything else
on Planet Earth,
it has struggled
to shake off the mud,
creep steadily to the surface
and reach toward the sun.

The Greening of George

Have you outstript the rest? Are you the President? It is a trifle. They will more than arrive there, every one, and still pass on. - Walt Whitman

When the gravesite preparations
for one George W. Bush become necessary,
the place should be marked with empty liters
of Pennzoil—hundreds of them.

George will expect them to bloom like Spring flowers,
just as he told us that waves of wheat
would sprout from all the blood in the sand
he helped to spread. No roots will take hold at his site,
and the sun will never shine in the bone-colored sky.

Neptune's Eye

Early bloom in the desert after a winter of saturation:
cactus rose in every crevice, wildflowers abundant as scrub-grass,
wind and rain from Tierra del Fuego to the Brooks Range in Alaska,
flash floods, mud slides, swells lined up like dominoes—
in Laguna Beach, a man found half a ton of green jade,
rare as starfish on these shores.

Green jade made the news, and I wondered why we marvel
at shiny treasures, meek astonishments, we foot creatures with thin covers
dry as chaparral, awed by jewelry covered in wet sand,
and yet we lack the deep blue imagination to sink down
fathom after fathom to Neptune's purple eye, a universe below
where we don't even know the habits of the squid.

Instead, we gaze up, looking to expand, losing subliminal sounds
vocabulary of leviathans, original mind lost on the sea floor
buried beneath our feet,
and the silent foam playing upon our toes agonizes,
wave after wave, like a repentant father who can't express himself.

Everything's written in Sanskrit of salt, dreams revealed in our palms
like holy explanations if we could only connect the lines,
shadow of whale
dolphin's perfect curve
iodine of forefathers
goddess face in swells.

Atlantis was nothing—
you should see what's further down.

Time of the Year

October is Santa Ana's time—
listen to her gust across the desert
and shudder through passes
like a wave of sand
returning to the coast.
Earth cracks in her wake,
skin dries out like baked clay.

Sweet Saint Ann boils the sea breeze
with fire and turbulence,
and at the end of her exhausting day,
she explodes across the sky
in a suicidal pose
for all the world to see—
fire red yellow sun
burning orange wax,
painter's pallet in the sky.

This is what we are,
angry cool colors
steaming to higher ground,
primary as earthquakes.
At this time of year, everything shakes,
the year is old, but she's got something left.
Listen to her scream—
it's not a death knell, it's the lungs of the wind
primal and punctual.
The wind is never late,
none of us ever are.

Heaven All Around Us

As the moon moves closer and waxes on my shoulders
like a second face, as if I were another sphere
among a thousand other moons, I try to take stock:

I believe this electric brain is nothing more than a rhythmic pulse
which beams ahead or lags behind, and might be traced if we had
the knack. I believe we are the sum parts of brilliant energy

lodged in bone marrow and blood, leaking like sap from branches
on the tree of life, with generations of salves to stanch the past—
and yet we are a muddled botch of clay,

blind as drunks at closing time, timid as a passing glance, we creatures
of weak skin and eye teeth, no different than our genes or capillaries.
And on a floating orb, we sail through expanding space like hybrid seeds

rejected from their soil, casting for anchors to slow the mortal fall
as if we didn't know a billion years of darkness will never yield
the light we seek, which doesn't mean it isn't there.

Moving, always moving, even in death we move along the shores
of space and draw defining lines that separate the distance
from all the rest of us, and it occurs to me:

like arrows with faulty shafts doomed to miss their mark,
we're moving through these waves of space with heaven all around us
disappearing as we pass.

Tidal Waves

As a child, I dreamed of tidal waves,
tsunami not yet in our lexicon,
and in these dreams the waves passed through me
as if I were incorporeal, a shadow on the sand;
I felt the soothing spray
and the power of the liberating sea,
but none of its mythology of fear.

A child in *Aceh* had the same dreams
until one day a rumbling on the ocean floor
separated the sea from its moorings,
and the sea took back the shorelines,
and thousands of humans became fossils
as if a million years had passed in a single day.

Dreams and nightmares swam side by side
gasping for breath
begging the trees to hold them,
and if you look closely into the evening sky,
you will see that constellations are made of bones
all the stars are fish,
and the ocean never ends.

Trusting the Moon

The strangeness of this solitary room has magnified
now that everything has shrunk:
the bed sold, books, shelves, pictures scuttled,
so many things have grown wings and flown away;
six years within these walls, spider webs untouched
insect legs hanging by strings.

Outside, the sea carries memories—
they wash out with waves and float back in
diminished, yet they have grown.
The waves are figments of dreamers,
they talk me to sleep, one will bury me
when the tides peak; the sea wears me down,
wears the world down.
We are smooth stones shrinking under her feet,
pebbles tossed in her trough—
tonight, my love tastes like salt, I am bleached sand;
tonight, I will glide past the break line,
a prisoner of tides. Tonight, I will venture further out
and trust the moon to pull me back.

Growl
for the Neocons

I saw the worst minds of my generation devour greed and hubris
like voracious locusts eating their young, colder than street
hustlers selling themselves for dime bags, knowing they carry
disease. I saw the planet left for dead, with all its holy estuaries
and tall trees sold to half-human, half-microchipped, fat-assed
corporate scum afraid to show face or run naked in the woods,
afraid to even run away. I saw the worst minds of my generation
get jilted of innocence by lust for power, and then spend the
rest of their lives trying to cover up the raw facts of their
uselessness; enraged by impotence, lack of creativity, inability
to love, psychotic selfishness, unrelenting pain, suburbanized
and sanitized to a point where they can't even get the blues. I
saw the worst minds of my generation attempt to turn the whole
world into monitor heads with all our body parts on-line and
for sale. I saw them mix religion and country music side-by-side
on cable TV, don't matter which one you believe in s'long as
you can two-step to both. I saw them divide great nations into
haves and have-nots, safe havens or toxic wastelands, housed or
homeless, cared for or filed away. I saw all of this and screamed
naked and bloody on a street corner and no one even looked.
I'm just a crazy hep-cat poet with ridiculous visionary dreams.
I'm just a see-through artist with no lines left to define.

Coffee Poem

We got mixed blends
from around the world,
we got coffee for your head;
we got coffee that'll getcha girls
& coffee to getcha wed—
we got hazelnut & smokeweed
gnarly zap & Alaska Red,
oil-pump & petrol-steam
& coffee bringin' back the dead—
we got capos & espressos
& Zimbabwe Tribal Hooch,
razzy jazzbeans & excessos,
caffeine kibbles for your pooch.
We got aspen tint & pine tree green
(mix 'em together make ya feel obscene)
we got day-glo blue from Kalamazoo
that'll separate your feet from your shoes—
we got coffee that'll make you bald
or grow your hair clear down to your knees,
coffee that'll make your Maker call
or turn your tongue to ripe bleu cheese,
we got coffee to make you run all day
coffee that'll make you gulp Tokay
coffee that'll make you roll in the hay
or bend your knees and start to pray,
coffee that'll make you percolate
coffee to help you circulate
coffee that'll make you work real late,
we got COFFEE, folks
and that's no joke—
an' if you don't believe me
then stick to herb tea.

Planet of War

I saw a frozen soldier, stiff as an ice floe, propped up on tundra
by his combat gear as though at rest, boots filled with snow,
blue lipped, the brows above his eyes crusted with frost,
skin drawn and bleached like driftwood, gun stuck
to his hands, and his bayonet thrust at my chest
as if I had startled him.

And in this last pose he looked so gruesome, so casually obscene,
not even made-up yet for the grave. I knew his face and name,
I knew he would crumble like the yoke of a parched egg.
I knew he had been there for millions of years
and I knew that nothing had changed.

His tribe was all around me, we had the same names,
we'd held hands in school, gone to war, had the same dreams.
His feet were firmly hooked to the ground, clamped by tree roots
that rose to claim him. He was already germinating.

The ghosts of mankind had torn his guilt apart,
left him sagging like a patch of straw with bare strings
holding the heft of his life, but all the air had puffed out.
The eye of his mind was as blind as the lines on his hands.

I watched him resurrect like a plant stretching to the sun,
float like pollen in desolate cold,
and vanish into long, gray clouds.

Asteroid Children
for Misty Mallory

There is a great spirit in my conception
of time, space, vacuums
and dreams; it's a shape changer
a trickster, a rock, and we're particles.
It's a boulder and we're smithereens,
knicked shavings turned to dust on a whim,
banished from our plans in the next avalanche,
be it meteor or mountain.

Sometimes we are no more than scree
at the base of a granite slide
baking in ultraviolet sun, waiting for glaciers
to pass; sometimes we think there is form
and gaze into space, as if what is not there
will eventually transform. Be happy if you achieve
a level of stone because that is ascension.
People will slip on your trail,
no footprints are left behind,
it's easy to pass through time,
and the wind will laugh from four corners
like an old, distant friend.

Death Card

So old Father Death is comin'
round your mountain when he comes,
and you want me to be shocked and awed?
I see his tired old bones and stupid skull face
every Halloween
and all you do is give him pagan sweets.
Hell, he's never even climbed his own mountain,
preferring to hide in caves
like a religious freak,
and he loves to get your juices going
when he saddles his horse for a ride.

Come here, Father Death,
come here to daddy,
give me a big sloppy kiss.
At least I can close my mouth;
all you can do is smile.

Looking Back to See Ahead

I talk to silent brothers killed in Vietnam,
buried alive with orange cancer at 22,
homeless on the streets in purgatory
or chained to bedpans forever,
abandoned by the nation they loved.

I tell them I'm alive but not at peace—
I defied America, burned the flag,
stopped the war machine, blew the minds
of slack old men whose liver-spotted hands
fondled rockets and bombs, who signed away
the blood of youth as if it were desert sand.
I tweaked the skulls at the Pentagon
and exposed their leather masks.

I took a stand against a war no one would declare,
and I am moving under your feet in silence
like a tectonic plate, ready to shatter.
I am thin glass, I am black ice,
I am waiting to shake.

I say to dead brothers in the Nam
and to my namesake, shot dead in another war:
I am taking you home to my temple of prayers,
I have balm for your wounds, music of the spheres.
I have tonics and potions, I am taking you home,
I am taking you home.

Evy's Yard

Tall rose in backyard
stretches blood red to the moon
and reports the day:

what the doves were up to,
why mockingbirds squabbled with crows,
the strange marauding parrots
plundering like huns,
and all the greens sway back and forth
in silent conversations,

gardenia and moonflower
snow drop and the glads
amaryllis and hibiscus
aloes with the mums.
In the corner, jacaranda
lays down a purple path,
night blooming jasmine
stands quiet in the drive,
wise old carob tree waits.

A kingdom of silence
gathers by moonlight,
sinewy roots
churning through the night.

Growing Peace

Mix tranquil words
with silent tears,
    churn bloody grounds
    into fields of soy,
grow flowers in every urn,
change fervid sand into fertile soil.
    Plant the past
    like a new born seed.

If you harbor ships of hatred,
release them to the sea
unfurl the sails lovingly
    freedom's in salt air
    peace is in the rudder.

    Listen closely
the waves beneath your ship never repeat themselves,
yet they constantly speak.

If you miss their whispered sounds
you will miss the nourishment
in their tones.
You've never had this conversation,
    it may not come again.

The Big Screen

What will it take to appreciate this tiny blue planet, smaller than an eyelash in real space and time, tiny blue planet moving in a perpetual vacuum of violence and destruction in this whacked-out part of the universe? Here in the green desert, most folks bow their heads and turn away from the chaos going on around them twenty-four hours a day, and they go to fantasy stores larger than the churches where they worship science fiction and fairy tales, fantasy stores filled with cheap stuff made by slave labor, and they buy ever-larger screens than the ones they just bought, with even more programming and more channels and more games, and they root for home teams in towns where they have no roots, and they watch the end of the world on their big screens and pretend that all this insanity is really happening in a different part of the world billions of light years away and is therefore not their problem, and the only problem here is a simple one of deciding whether to change the channel to a new fantasy or follow this one through, but the people on this tiny blue planet, planet of liquid, planet where every living thing is dependent upon water, don't even know where their water comes from, and they don't care, and in fact they don't view this as a problem because their water is pre-packaged and pre-treated, just like their food, like all their products, like their very lives which don't really exist because religions teach that someone else is directing them in the movie of themselves on the big screen from the big store under the big sky where the big fairy tales come from, and no one cares when the movie ends as long as their names are listed in big letters scrolling down in the credits at the end of the big movie that no one ever sticks around to see.

The Vocabulary of Stars

Here we are again, we strange, disconnected beings,
multi-layered with spirit molecules, souls ignited
by sparks, hearts kindled in fire, minds born of sea water,
breathing primeval air in an outback of the universe,
roving an alien planet, lost and lonely, searching for signs
of the asteroids from whence we came, our sunken
memories stuffed with legends and stories
of astral travel, journeys through space and time;
and all the ciphers and petroglyphs left behind
hark back to our beginnings
when words weren't needed
voices were mute
brains were brim full,

and the vocabulary of stars
was the language of the universe,
and never was there a need
to sound a description,
never was there a need
to write something down.

The Impossibility of Death

Written for the Winter Solstice, 2010 "Gathering of the Tribes" party at BC Space Gallery in Laguna Beach

Take my hand, friend. I've got my visa stamped for the undiscovered country, and so do you. Let's go down the rabbit hole, and we'll close our eyes along the way. It's *beautiful*, isn't it? The sheer speed of this ride, the tsunami wash of space, the thrill of unimaginable freedom, the shackles of the body peeling off like rust, slipping away like quicksilver, while asteroids and comets cascade past us as fast as we cascade forward into the vastness, into beautiful blackness at last, at long last, pure spirit, the feeling of being not *in* the universe, but *around* it, being *all* of the universe, everything open and revealed, no compass and no direction, more colors and energies in the blackness than can be named or conjured, the five senses becoming ten, and then a billion, and then sextillion, and the endless beaming of *welcome home!* from the teeming stars. *Congratulations!* You've done it, you're free, your loved ones are up ahead, and yet they are here, every one of them, all your dogs, cats, your horse, your totems; all of your imagination is here. *Can you feel it?* Yes, and they are just as much a part of everything as you are, and none of us can ever reach the edge of the universe because there is no end, no edge from which to fall...and it's *so* beautiful, this feeling, filled to the brim at last and yet as empty as a cloud, and nothing matters because everything *is* matter. And we consider things like a solar eclipse or a meteor shower or a bottomless lake or a UFO to be astonishing! We consider our self-bordered significance to be the sum of our senses, and yet there is a drop of water outside on a blade of grass, one out of billions of others, and that drop of water is the imbuement of us, the shadows in our brains, our whole imprint. It is the sum of all our mysterious love, all we long for, all we are, all we've been—all we'll ever need to be.

Monk's Paradise

Lie down, love,
lie down and dream with me
on my floating mattress on the floor,
so close to the shore
that it shakes like a raft at sea
when large swells rumble in;
this is my universe—no furniture—
just a lamp that sits atop
an upturned flower pot,
a monk's paradise where I dream
not of the Diamond Sutra, but of you,
and if I seem a bit strange
remember it was you who said,
"Pisces sun and Scorpio moon,
do your feet ever touch the ground?"

Of course not—like Walt Whitman,
I am a cosmos unto myself
and you are right—
I can't feel the earth beneath my feet,
but I will show you oceans
we can walk across.

IV Mixed Bag

Crossing the Street in Laguna Beach

Thank you for not killing me in the metal-grilled cross-hairs
of your monstrous SUV as I crossed the street
cautiously, in full view, in daylight, in the cross-walk
where I thought I had a lawful right to be
and indeed once did in a different, slower world
when I could meander and even take a peek upward
at a trail of pelicans
or outward at a glorious pod of dolphins,
but now I must deal with the likes of you
as you fight for space, wrecking the world
with anger
and the awful weight of your toys.

Hwy 395

Hitchhiking down 395 with a good friend in 1969: dusty
rucksacks, empty pockets, deflated dreams, Vietnam raging,
same year as the moon landing, Woodstock, Altamont, Manson,
My Lai revelations, end of The Beatles, endless Nixon—also
with us my Malamute pup whose first three months were spent
in the back country chasing deer, and we're down from the
mountains headed south, long-haired freaks looking like John
Muir, wild-eyed and uncivilized, with a wolf-like creature as
their companion, no one's going to give us a ride and I can't
blame them, and we walk from Mammoth all the way to Lone
Pine, or so it seems, late August sun blazing away—we're in the
tired, slump-shouldered dejection that only hitchhikers can
truly appreciate—throw out your thumb with no enthusiasm and
don't even turn around, why bother; and a beat up car pulls over
(euphoria!) and, as if anyone will believe this, it's an old friend
from Reno with cold beer and hashish on his way to L.A. and it's
snug in the car, but we settle in laughing, puffing, and chugging
all the way, and we can't believe our good luck. Our dreams
rekindle; anything's possible, Nixon's an illusion, everything is—
but I carry Mono Lake, as well as Burro, Summit, and Hook Lakes in
my canine soul and coyote heart, and the glacial scars and craggy
pines in the High Sierras are etched in my memories, notched on
my skin like veins, purple lupine forever blooming in my brain—
wild onions in the frying pan, fish rising on the lakes in early
dawn all these millions of years.

Cosmic Sex

As the sun gave a sexy, sideways wink
from the corner of his saffron eye
and disappeared behind Catalina Island,
someone said, "Watch for the flash of green
at his nadir point," which I didn't see,

but I like the idea of the sun waving goodbye
and quickly changing into a solar powered,
tight-fitting, green suit—ahhh yes,
that sly old playboy,
posing manfully in the west
and flashing those fiery tresses
before flexing his way to a hot date

with the moon, that minx of a moon
who fools no one with her wanderlust
and just wants the sun to herself
to do unto him as she will.

Poetry Reading at a Retirement Village

What an unexpected blessing
to hear a WWII vet at a senior center
read one of his poems today
about crashing his plane during the war:
ten on board, only four survived.
During the rest of the reading
he sat slumped by his walker, snoring softly,
that special napping of the very old,
open-mouthed, as if surprised to be alive.
With all the sleeping taking over,
the waking will soon fade away,
and he was followed by a 99-year-old
woman who, before reading her poem,
winked at the old vet and said:

Plane crashes ain't nothing, sonny!
I crashed and burned at Dachau,
but somehow rose like a phoenix from the ashes
and flew over the ovens, and I've been
flying ever since. You can clip my wings
all you want, but it won't stop me.
I've been to the end of the sky
and I'm still flying.

Language of the Leaves

This page in my journal has stain marks
from serving as a coaster for yet another Pilsner beer
as I work on getting wasted at the Chronos Bar
in the Clarion Congress Hotel in Prague, and yet
I feel an immense satisfaction in mindless word-doodling
instead of listening to the ungrateful dead upstairs, one dreary
academician after another droning away, one dreary
Power Point presentation after another on the white boards
of higher education that fascinates only the professor
who currently has the floor.

Ah! There's Filomena, the hot Czech mathematician,
looking just as guilty as me for skipping out, sipping
late morning Bloody Marys, but I won't flirt with her today
because I feel like a strange old coot stranded on a sand bar
of isolation and dead words, and she's staring at a gadget
in her hand, and I think I'm the only person on the planet
who isn't staring at an I-Pad, You-Pad, We-Pad, They-Pad,
Me-Pad, We-All-Pad, a world of scrolling and texting.

If I were back in Laguna Canyon, I'd be listening
to the sound of ginkgo leaves sprinkling my roof
like rain drops in the wild Santa Ana winds, *ginkgo biloba*,
a living fossil, dating back to the early Jurassic, healer
of circulatory problems and an aid to memory functions.
Six of them survived the Hiroshima bombing and are still alive,
and their deciduous sounds from the pre-ice age,
the pitter-patter language of swirling leaves, is the only one
I care to hear.

Lasting Peace through Lasting Death

Make way for the funeral march of endangered species
in Iraq—call out to those who are leaving.
Wave goodbye to the Socotra cormorant, the white-headed
duck, the marbled teal, imperial eagle, kestrel,
lapwing warbler, little grebe, sand plover, curlew, white-cheeked
tern, even the wild goat.

Make way for the wilderness of uranium:
bullets, tanks, shells, bombs,
and a fresh coating of oxide dust.
Say hello to the mighty Cruise Missile,
wave goodbye to the Greater-Spotted Eagle.

A small boy walks down the bleached streets
of Fallouja and asks his father,
What kind of birds are those?
His father answers,
Those, my son, are helicopters and drones. They eat
all the other birds in our sky and bring us lasting peace
through lasting death.

Dog Prose

For hours I putter about the garden, head down like a man
looking for something he's lost; a key, a coin, perhaps an abstract
thought. The dogs follow dutifully, sniffing in my tracks, tails
wagging, glancing up with big serious wondrously soulful
eyes, carefully scratching away top soil, crusts of clay and thin
surfaces of salt, the mighty sea a stone's throw away—they dig
into a prehistoric past, odor of dinosaur and leviathan down
below, shiny noses hundreds of times more powerful than mine,
hoping to be my heroes and find what I'm seeking. They live
in a different dimension, one where opossums and raccoons
are the size of wildebeests. Surely my task is important, and the
very safety of the garden is at stake. They scoot about furiously,
covering my back, eager to root out this problem, noses skating
just above the ground. Perhaps aliens are already here, blending
into the world of earwigs, ants, and sow bugs. We would never
know, and what marvelous camouflage. And the safety in
numbers! We'll never match their populations. They already
control our planet—but the dogs know everything is under
control. They know I'm simply pacing out my time, intent on
nothing—and staring, sniffing, or puttering is as good a path
as any. They know that nothing really needs to be done. T'ang
master Lin Chi said: "In Buddhism, there is no place for using
effort. Just be ordinary and nothing special. Eat your food, move
your bowels, pass water, and when you're tired go and lie down.
The ignorant will laugh at me, but the wise will understand."
Ah, my little Buddha dogs, indulging my ignorant activities,
bored now and returning to their napping meditations, much
closer to enlightenment than I am. Out here in the garden
among the bright, blooming flowers and the sun-hidden stars
and the sound of changing tides, all I have to do is bloom, as do
the dogs and the insects, everything blooming, even as we go to
seed, and then to bloom again.

My Home on the Planet

We are such stuff as dreams are made on, and our little life is rounded with a sleep. – Shakespeare

When visiting my small A-Frame in the forest—
borrowed furniture, old mattress on the floor,
wood stove designed by my grandfather
and a lifetime's accumulations
easily fitting within this space—
friends are amazed how little I have.

I came into the world with nothing
and will leave with the same.
Everything I have is a prop
on the stage of my time in this play,
and even the character I've been assigned
will leave his costume at the door.

Wolf Mountain

Box cars of fog slowly wind around Wolf Mountain
like a ghost train painted on silk screen,
and then the rains come and the ghost train
disappears, and then here she comes again,
comin' round the mountain, and the engineer
is an old zen lunatic poet, drunk and happy
with a crinkly smile and a face like dry moss,
and his lips are burgundy, and he yells out:

"Ain't it great to realize this is all there is?
That's YOU over there in the corner,
just now getting painted into being!"

And the Child Danced
for Devin Cohee

She was the dervish in the room,
dancing around the poets' words
as if she had been conjured
by the metaphors of *Calliope*.

She never wavered
between the sunbeam's ciphers
and the moonlight's figures of speech,
the music of words, words, words,

the music of the *sphere* of words,
as if she were saying,
This is how everyone speaks,
this is the language of the world.

How did the child know?
How did she become preternatural?
How do we flounder through our dictionaries
without her dance of syllables?

The cadence of the ocean's waves
is the rhythm of our sounds,
and that is where you'll find the child,
teaching the tides to dance.

Third Class Rail

What a bad idea that was—
"I'll save money," I had told myself,
crossing the Sahara desert in the baggage car
crammed in with goats, sacks of onions
and *Minianka* tribesmen on their way
to the mud mosques of Mopti, Mali.
They offered coffee-colored water
which I gladly accepted, 120 degrees outside
and of course dysentery would hit later, before
the mosquitoes, some the size of small bees,
would inject malaria into my veins,

and when I got to Bamako
my thighs were blistered with heat rashes
and I was covered with bugs and fleas
and couldn't stop twitching,
crazy American with long hair
in an ancient desert where nothing's changed
in a thousand years, and I've got the jitters
and a fever, scratching and sweating,

and this is how it will end, me slumped over my dusty
backpack, felled by one disease or another,
a few locals whispering in the native language
of *Bambara* before releasing my carcass
to the hot sands and desert winds in the land
of Timbuktu, picked over by vultures, just like any other
fool in the desert, wide-eyed and unprepared, soon to be
smooth white bones, sun bleached and wind-washed,
broken into pieces, painted with brilliant colors,
and used as trading beads passed from hand to hand
until they disappear in the desert sand.

Waves and Shores

How can one describe
the sound of wind through pine trees?
After many years by the sea,
it sounds to me like an ebbing tide.

Clouds come and then recede
guided by firm reins of the wind—
waves bounce back and forth
along many coasts,
pushed by gusts from the four corners
of our blue globe,
and most of this is still mysterious.

How to describe shooting stars,
meteors and asteroids
from whence we came?

Perhaps our fathers were distant waves
and our mothers were the shores.

Janis

Streaking comet
burning through
our atmosphere,
jet-streams *ON*

Hard to figure
if she was landing
or trying to return
dem mean ol' kozmic blues
back to the sea of space.

Empty Arms

We fell into each other's empty arms because there was so much heavenly space to be found there—room upon room filled with romantic literature, gallant tales of lords and ladies, fairy tale endings, a front porch with towering magnolias growing next to redwoods, silkweed and eglantine, brilliant tones of lantern glow, like colored gauze on scrim cloth, soft as the morning sun peeking from its eastern perch and covering spirits of the rivers with refracted light, a diary with our names and confessions of loneliness side by side, finally free from the expanse of bordered pages, and now there is nothing else to do—we have ethereal love that doesn't need the realm of ether, we are uncontained, we are stellar songs unto ourselves, which is all the music we will need.

Sunday Morning

On a beautiful Sunday morning, I salute birds—
stellers and scrub-jays, red-tailed hawks, even the vulture
who, while not so radiant,
still makes graceful circles in the updrafts
and creates an imprint I don't understand
yet nurtures my needs.

The Bible thumpers and sellers of screeds
are in downtown churches, and their words also circle
in windy updrafts of pomp and custom,
rustle around stained glass windows
and fill the assembled worshipers with enough guilt
for the long, sinful week ahead.

I don't know if there are really angels in the sky,
but I do believe in creatures with wings—
they're already half-way to the next world.

The Spider

The spider I killed this morning, walking across my bed sheet, deserved a better fate. It wasn't a brown recluse or wolf spider, and it certainly wasn't a daddy long legs or innocuous species from the garden, but I'd already disposed of two black widows earlier in the week. Usually, I capture spiders in a cup or glass and release them outdoors in the best spirit of doing no harm. This time I reacted before thinking, and I wonder how many times that has happened to the sleep-deprived soldier, surprised by a comrade in a jungle filled with sudden venom. Perhaps this is a bad comparison, but death is death, my hand was involved, and my prayers and thoughts go out to this spider just as surely as they would to any other living being, now making its way into what we can only hope is a less entangled world.

Tunnels of Song

Whales sing their songs to other mammals half-way around the
world. They follow their songs through water just as we do on land.
–Aboriginal Myth

I dreamed that whales have been singing high pitched songs
half-way around the world to other Cetaceans for millions of
years, tunnels of song many fathoms down, uninterrupted by
storms, tides or rogue waves, from one ocean to another, far
more advanced than our primitive sonar, and I traveled with
them in my blue imagination, barnacle-clad as the rest, singing
near the Canary Islands, a response from Cape Horn, a message
from the Sea of Japan, another from Madagascar, songs of
plain things, feeding and breeding grounds, and they spoke of
immense waterfalls miles below the ocean's surface that defy our
skimpy mathematics, and they spoke of a Whale Elder living
at the bottom of the sea near Antarctica beneath mountains of
steel-blue ice, unseen and silent except for its songs, controlling
temperatures on land and sea, taking back our coastlines with
quakes and tsunamis until we learn that *dominion* does not mean
superior, and the Elder's songs told of more years to pass before
humans burn their useless negativity and learn to kindle light
in the universe below; it spoke of cruel beings who kill whales,
the genies of the sea, never bothering to understand Cetacean
vocabulary and the simple secrets that could change us all—
the Elder speaks with every fish in the sea and knows every
language on land, and it watches us and sighs and sighs as we
feverishly probe the Black Sea, a landscape of silt and bacteria,
for Noah's Ark and oil. We grind away time and fill our dreams
with ignorance, missing what's inside us—the bottom of the
ocean is inside, just listen to the cranial waves, the water-time
continuum, it's all inside. We've been expected for centuries,
and we don't even have to open our eyes.

Flight

Same blur of bodies in all the airports of the world,
faceless, ambulatory beings indistinguishable
one from the other, same reverberating language,
veil of clucking tongues and metered grunts,
belongings rolling behind, ticket clutched
as if one's life depended on it,
and then we all fly away.

And the planet also flies, spins us to destinations
we've always sensed, pulses through the cosmos
at speeds defying gravity, all of us on board,
tickets preordained. *This* is the only flight that matters,
the constant passage, the passport stamp of galaxies
we visit in our dreams yet don't understand,
the language of space and time, of the quiet canyon,
the bottom of the sea, the sound you're making now
in the silence of this room.

Forever Haiti

A vast parabola of spinning planets
streaking asteroids and falling stars,
showers of meteors, an expanding universe,
moon pulling from above,
tectonic plates grinding below,
we mark our time by luck and happenstance
while catastrophes shatter our clocks and plans.

There are explanations for quakes and tsunamis,
but not for the mother digging with her bare hands
to free her child trapped beneath the aftermath.
No matter where you are, something is homing in,
be it the sting of disease or collapsing roof.

Nature is as moody as the rest of us
and for all the shining diamond days she brings,
she also serves a poisoned broth of chaos in the night.
In one way or another
at some time and in some place,
we are all Haitians.

Ghost Nets

I thought *ghost nets* must be incantations
from shamans or instructions given by bodhisattvas,
or the totem dance of medicine men and brujos,
or perhaps the lateral loops of a desert spider's
web, built to withstand the strongest Washoe wind—
instead, they're simply gillnets on continental slopes
drifting in the ocean, abandoned or dumped,
lost in a locus of death,
thousands of kilometers worth (no one really knows
how many plague the sea beds), catching or ensnaring
marine life for years, ghost nets left by ghost people.

Perhaps in their next lives, in a world of karma
and equipoise, the ghost people will return as goldfish
staring bubble-eyed from glass prisons in bedrooms
of small children, forgetful of feeding,
pet goldfish plucked lifeless from the surfaces of bowls
and flushed down the toilets of the world.

The Marshlands
for Galway Kinnell

Old deaths wander
here, under green
sedgy plots

blue teals flutter by
in ones, curlews
huddle on bleak limbs—

the ground is
swollen
with dead compost

dry bones break through
wood coffins
and rise like plants.

Galway Kinnell was my poetry teacher at the University of California, Irvine in 1968 - '69. This is one of the few poems I wrote for his class that wasn't "beyond bad," or so I hope. He was a wonderful teacher and remains one of America's finest poets.

Ghana

In a dungeon room on the Gold Coast
where slaves were detained, cannon mounts
intact on crumbling walls, I think of those
who lay awake in misery and filth, destined
for work farms across the sea; I have nightmares
about an old woman whose bones were removed
and crushed like chalk, and she smiles
because now she can write the truth in her own pulp.

Waking with malaria, sweating through the mattress
and dripping from the springs, I create a lake of salt
shaped like a mosquito on the floor, and now I'm part
of the terrain; I hear the constant song of Ouagadougou,
my skin is made of Kenti cloth.

There is a lyric drum phrase rising from Africa
with the same regularity as the sun;
it thumps through rain forests, energizes banyan trees—
it's as old as stories of the hunt
and sings like a thunder storm
pelting banana leaves with pebbles of rain,
and lining the Indian Ocean
with grieving beads of sweat.

Diamond Thought

Nothing matters, nothing whatsoever, unless you have a shining diamond thought that rockets evolution forward by an iota, like a twig tossed into a fire that flames out and disappears, leaving a momentary curl of smoke, and if through good fortune you see through this smoke, someone else will recognize it, run with it, hang it above a mountain like a painting of a cloud filled not with the promise of rain, but the truth in water itself.

Acknowledgments

"Backyard Jungles" was published in prose, under a different title, in "Blue Arc West, An Anthology of California Poets," Tebot Bach, 2006

"Swimming to Catalina" was published under a different title in "Blue Satellite," Sacred Beverage Press, 2000

"Californian" was published in "So Luminous the Wildflowers, An Anthology of California Poets," Tebot Bach, 2003

"Back to the Sea," "Tidal Waves," and "Walking the Marin Rim with an Old Friend" were published in "Tide Pools, An Anthology of Orange County Poetry," Moon Tide Press, 2006

"Shadows of Themselves" was published under a different title in "Polluted Poems, An Anthology of Environmental Poems," Orange Ocean Press, 1994

"Enniskillen" and "Monk's Paradise" were published in "Interstices, An Anthology," Windflower Press, 2010

"Time of the Year" was published in "Incidental Buildings & Accidental Beauty, An Anthology of Orange County/Long Beach Poets," Tebot Bach, 2001

"Asteroid Children" was published in "Misty Mallory, Words in Praise and Appreciation," Aphasia Press, 2000

"The Cats of Leningrad" and "Kano to Cairo" were published in "The Hummingbird Review," a literary anthology, 2012

Many of these poems appeared, in different versions with different titles, in small collections published by The Inevitable Press and FarStarFire Press, Laguna Beach, CA, and North Star House Publishing, Berkeley, CA

About the Poet

 John Gardiner has published 10 collections of poetry and been published in numerous anthologies, journals and magazines, including two Anthologies of CA Poets (Tebot Bach), Spillway, The Sacred Beverage Press, Speakeasy, Write Bloody, Moon Tide Press, Poetry Flash (Berkeley), Windflower Press, CA Poetry Quarterly, Art Life, and The Comstock Journal. In addition to hundreds of featured readings in the U. S., Gardiner has also featured in Russia, The Czech Republic, Italy, Germany, Ireland, and Brazil. He tours in a rock 'n roll Shakespeare show called "Shakespeare's Fool" and has facilitated poetry readings, slams, and workshops in Laguna Beach for the past 16 years. Gardiner teaches Drama, Shakespeare and Oral Presentation for the Gifted Students Academy at U.C.I.